Hearts Forged in Resistance

poems by

Chella Courington

Finishing Line Press
Georgetown, Kentucky

Hearts Forged
in Resistance

ACKNOWLEDGMENTS

Versions of several poems originally appeared in the following works:

"Job's Daughter," *Mizmor L'David Anthology*
"Stigma," *I Am Not A Silent Poet*
"From Juárez," *Confluence*
"Good Trouble," *Valiant Scribe*
"Claudia Patricia Gomez Gonzalez Is Returned to Mother Earth," *Ethel*
"Light," *Scapegoat Review*
"I Spend Hours Killing Chickens," "Grief," & "Mama's Rug Is an Elegy I
Cannot Write," *Roi Fainéant Press*
"Ghost Ranch," *Sonic Boom & As Above So Below*
"Strength" & "Sláva Ukrayíni!," *The BeZine*
"Passage," *Purifying Wind*

Publisher: Leah Huete de Maines
Editor: Christen Kincaid
Cover Art: Robin M. Gowen
Author Photo: Ted Chiles
Cover Design: Elizabeth Maines McCleavy

Order online: www.finishinglinepress.com
also available on amazon.com

Author inquiries and mail orders:
Finishing Line Press
PO Box 1626
Georgetown, Kentucky 40324
USA

Table of Contents

Job's Daughter

I do not skulk from God   He has no lip for me
only for my father—tall and brown

Hurling insults like thunderbolts   God calls him *harelip*
Mooncalf   Father hides seven days under three sheep

God forces a camel to sit on the cold earth   head down
hands Father a flint   *Slice the thorax*   He bellows

Father turns away—not a butcher
The camel lives two hours   My father crawls inside

the camel's skin and folds it over him—flesh still warm

Stigma

Women are beaten—sometimes to death—writing poetry
My husband   maybe my father or brother   reads my emotion

spilling on the page   sees passion for a hidden lover
My burqa not enough to shield me

Just out of reach   I rub against silk and satin
turning inward to speak of loneliness—

tulip dying in the desert

Tremulous Heart

Caleb calls me sweetmeat   With cloth Sister Marie stuffs
his mouth & warns   *Don't let him touch you*

Sister Marie speaks softly   *Christ wants you spotless*
I want stigmata   She says they appear on *clean girls*

who never let boys   *play with their privates*   She catches
Caleb & me twisted together   forces me to kneel

on top of rice—digging into flesh   scouring every cell
No more nasty girl

Like angel wings her arms lift me   as she bends down
kissing my knees   blood smeared over trembling lips

From Juárez
(after a photograph by Miguel Gandert)

I'm Teresa Gutierrez   Look at me   Alive   Not like my friend
Cecilia Covarrubias
Shot once in each breast   tossed in a field where nothing grows

The next day I ask my cousin to work his magic   Tattoo the
Blessed Mother
clothed with stars and sun—spiked light down my back

He lines & shades   week after week   I flinch as our Lady of
Guadalupe rises
out of my jeans   I wear her to the maquiladora   to dark
crossroad   bus stops

Her mantle covers me

Good Trouble

Their clubs cracked your bones   Their tear gas
clogged your lungs   Their iron pipe almost ended your life

But you stood up   walked forward for fifty years plus more
When you died   the earth slowed   sun dimmed   air thinned

Yet we are not alone   You left us with your words
Walk with the wind   brothers and sisters   and let the spirit of peace

and the power of everlasting love be your guide

Claudia Patricia Gomez Gonzalez Is Returned to Mother Earth

Children cry in cages at the border   Drenched in dark dreams   I wake
My mother reaches from the grave   Nails catch the hem of my dress

I fall on granite   Red streaks my shins   Wrapped in a gray Mayan shawl
her mother sits silent   My father sobs   Dust spots his black suit

Dried red roses lay across his legs   Thorns pierce the wool   Her father
weeps
#Claudia Patricia Gomez Gonzalez   #Say her name   Just turned twenty

Taking flight from violence in Guatemala   Shot in the head by a Texas
border agent
May 23 2018   Her mother and father receive the white coffin   carrying
their daughter—

cover lifted partway

April Again

It rained everyday   floating seeds downstream
Cold white sheets covered cold
white skin & you said it was useless
caring whether hands met at night
You said in Poland   lovers lost
sleep over other things   We lay unspeaking
like the couple in Sunday's *LA Times*
She slept with his silence ten years then
burrowed a kitchen knife in his heart

I Spend Hours Killing Chickens

Not like Mom who swung the bird till the neck popped
My machine chops off the head   splatters blood—salty & sweet

The line chief brags he can smell a girl *on the rag*
Thursday he says he dreams of eating me

I don't tell him my dream—the hook curls through his neck
rips his vessels as he swings toward me—handling the blade

Light

In fingerless gloves   I thread the eye
pray   for easy passage

Glint from the silver thimble   reminds
me of glow worms   in a Georgia summer

specks of light   on pinewood
brown iris   rimmed in white

I long to be   above the factory glare
where sunlight   rolls through mist

Grief

My dad built biceps   working for US Steel   smelting iron
in heat that humbled men   Now I could break his arm

brittle as kindling   over my knee   My dad used to let me walk
up his body   balancing my hands on his fingertips   till I flew

from his shoulders   They began to sag after my mom fell
no moon out   and died while he slept   My dad saved the hair

from her brush   wrapped in Kleenex   stored in a wooden box
beside their bed   Every night he rubs strands against his cheek

Mama's Rug Is an Elegy I Cannot Write

Lush red wool   bordering blue hydrangeas
her rug unfurls at night

By morning loose strands scatter   I gather them
in a glass bowl   once holding goldfish won at a fair

I weave abandoned threads   into a mourning shawl
pray for her return

Resilience

It's the tumor remembered
cut from my breast

my breast chiseled from my bone
rising in dreams

or at the margins of whispered denial
when   startled   I feel it

how it might   again   pull at my nipple
and slip through my ribs

like a cat prowling

Ghost Ranch

Living in this forsaken land is unimaginable until
I see shadows   on desert hills   think of Georgia O'Keeffe

traveling across New Mexico   water colors dislodging dark
New York   her lover old enough to be her father   posing her

day after day in his studio   infatuations in black & white
Stieglitz dies   She escapes to open plains   sky vistas

no camera traps   no skyscraper blocks   her stretching into
whiteness
bone on red hills

Passage

I find a dead hawk   body's still warm
and take off to preserve the remains

Careful as a shaman   I wash him
bone by bone   douse quills in alcohol

store his down   in a cedar box
invoke his spirit   to stay seven days

until the body is at rest

Strength

I buy sunflowers today   fuzzy faces   canary yellow petals
stand them   one by one   sturdy stalks in an azure vase

7000 miles away   tanks roll across Ukrainian borders
trying to wipe them off the map

grandmothers   aunts   fathers   sons
throw their bodies against bully armor

hearts forged   in resistance

Sláva Ukrayíni!

Zelenskyy takes off his suit   puts on battle fatigues
stands in the streets   talks with his troops

And when his fellow patriots can't see him   literally
he makes videos—calls to soldiers from every continent

Russia turns its fire on Zaporizhzhia—home to
Europe's largest nuclear plant   six reactors   Flaming

shells like falling stars   cut into darkness   One orange
globe   lights up the sky   explodes beside a car park

We will not lay down our weapons   Our weapons are our truth

With a Ph.D. in British and American literature and an MFA in Poetry, **Chella Courington** is a writer and teacher who's published nine chapbooks of poetry and four of fiction. Her many stories and poems appear in a range of journals and anthologies including *SmokeLong Quarterly, The Collagist,* and *New World Writing.* Her poetry has been nominated for Best of the Net and Best New Poets along with awarded individual prizes, the most recent of which is Writing in a Woman's Voice Moon Prize for her poem "Eurydice." Her fiction also has been nominated for Best of the Net, Best Small Fictions, and Pushcart as well as awarded individual prizes, the most recent of which is the *Shooter Magazine* Flash Prize for "Showtime." She lives in Southern California with another writer and two feline boys. Twitter: *@chellacouringto* Instagram: *chellacourington*

www.ingramcontent.com/pod-product-compliance
Lightning Source LLC
Chambersburg PA
CBHW022110080426
42734CB00009B/1554